# MEDICAL
# CHARITIES
## AND THEIR WORK

By

# JOANNA BRUNDLE

©2018
Book Life
King's Lynn
Norfolk PE30 4LS

**ISBN:** 978-1-78637-312-0

**Written by:**
Joanna Brundle

**Edited by:**
Kirsty Holmes

**Designed by:**
Gareth Liddington

A catalogue record for this book
is available from the British Library.

**Photocredits: Abbreviations: l-left, r-right, b-bottom, t-top, c-centre, m-middle. All images are courtesy of Shutterstock.com.**

Cover – Africa Studio, 1 – stockcreations, 2 – Romaset, 3 – Boris Ryaposov, 4 – artistan, 5 – vectorfusionart, 6 – Gorodenkoff, 7 – Pavel Kubarkov, 8 – wavebreakmedia, 9 – Andrey_Popov, 10 – sirtravelalot, Maxispor, 11 – Mr Pics, 12 – XiXinXing, 13 – MediaGroup_BestForYou, 14 – Photographee.eu, 15 – Tony Baggett, 16 – malost, 17 – ChooChin, 18 – Oksana Kuzmina, 19 – Barry Barnes, 20 – steve bridge, 21 – Africa Studio, 22 – Rawpixel.com, 23 – Zurijeta, 24 – antoniodiaz.

Images are courtesy of Shutterstock.com. With thanks to Getty Images, Thinkstock Photo and iStockphoto.

All facts, statistics, web addresses and URLs in this book were verified as valid and accurate at time of writing. No responsibility for any changes to external websites or references can be accepted by either the author or publisher.

# CONTENTS

Words that look like **this** can be found in the glossary on page 24.

# WHAT IS A CHARITY?

A charity is an **organisation** that supports people, animals or **causes** that need help. Charities need to raise money in order to do this work.

THIS LADY IS COLLECTING MONEY FOR A CHARITY.

People who work for a charity without being paid are called volunteers.

Collecting money for charities is known as fundraising.

SOME MEDICAL CHARITIES CARRY OUT IMPORTANT RESEARCH INTO DISEASES.

There are thousands of charities around the world. Each charity helps a different group in need. Charities do not make a **profit**.

# WHAT DOES MEDICINE NEED?

THESE SCIENTISTS ARE TESTING A NEW MEDICINE.

Medical research is expensive. Money is needed for **laboratories** and equipment and to pay the scientists and doctors who carry out the research.

Research is very important because it helps scientists to discover new information about diseases. It also helps them to find cures and better **treatments**.

Medical research can take many years to complete.

SOME CHARITIES WORK WITH DRUG COMPANIES TO PRODUCE NEW MEDICINES.

# HOW DO MEDICAL CHARITIES HELP?

Medical charities raise money and use it to set up research projects. Some give help and support to patients and families affected by a disease.

MEDICAL RESEARCH HELPS DOCTORS TO **DIAGNOSE** AND TREAT DISEASES.

THESE PEOPLE ARE LEARNING HOW TO HELP SOMEONE WITH A HEART PROBLEM.

Medical charities try to educate people about serious diseases. They give advice about what causes diseases and how they can be prevented.

# HOW DO MEDICAL CHARITIES RAISE MONEY?

Celebrities, like Mo Farah, often help charities to raise money.

Charities raise money by asking for **donations** online, on television and by using advertising posters. Some organise collections in the street or house-to-house.

The relatives of someone who has died from a serious disease may choose to make a donation. Sometimes they organise fundraising events in their memory.

Some charities organise nationwide fundraising events like coffee mornings.

THESE LONDON MARATHON RUNNERS ARE RAISING MONEY FOR DIFFERENT CHARITIES.

# HOW IS THE MONEY SPENT?

Money raised by medical charities pays for research and equipment. Some charities set up hospices that care for people near the end of their lives, or special hospital wards.

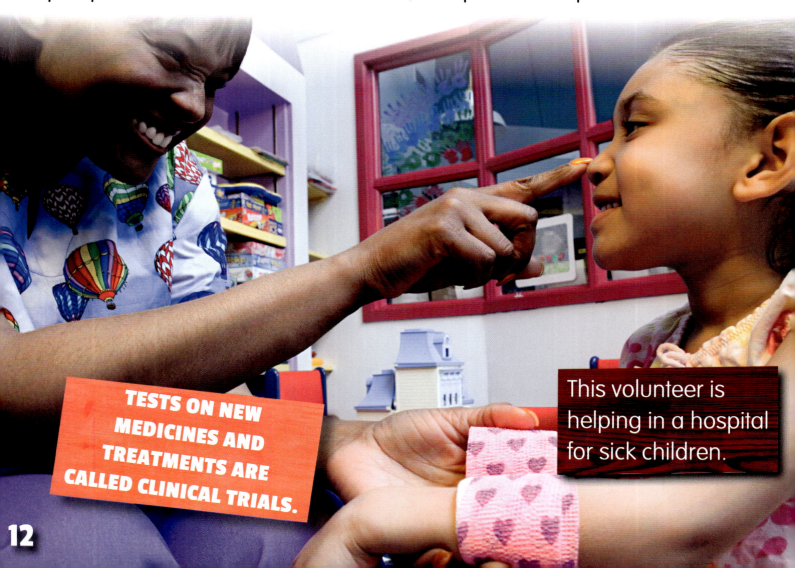

TESTS ON NEW MEDICINES AND TREATMENTS ARE CALLED CLINICAL TRIALS.

This volunteer is helping in a hospital for sick children.

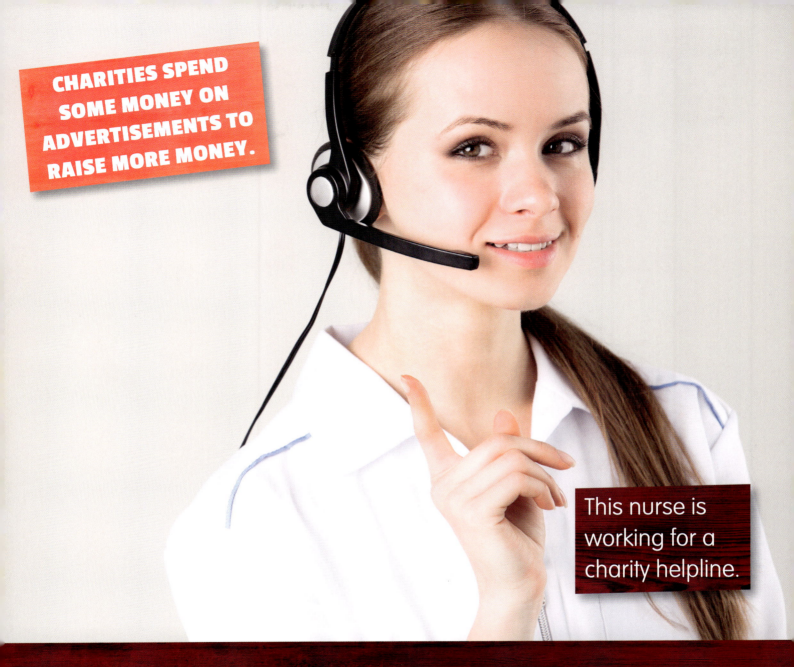

This nurse is working for a charity helpline.

Some medical charities pay for special nurses who look after sick people in their own homes. Some fund helplines that people can call for advice.

# SPARKS

**SPARKS IS FUNDING RESEARCH TO HELP CHILDREN WITH CYSTIC FIBROSIS.**

Sparks organises fundraising challenge events like cycle rides and sky-diving.

Sparks is a UK medical charity that began in 1991. It pays for research into serious illnesses that affect babies, children and mums-to-be.

Although Sparks is a UK charity, its research into diseases like epilepsy and arthritis has helped children across the world. Many celebrities help this charity.

Sparks has funded over 285 research projects in the UK.

Great Ormond Street Hospital for Children **NHS**
NHS Trust

**Great Ormond Street Hospital**

← **Ambulance Entrance**

**Main Entrance** →

SPARKS WORKS WITH THE WORLD-FAMOUS GREAT ORMOND STREET CHILDREN'S HOSPITAL.

# SMILE TRAIN

Smile Train is an international charity set up in 1999. It helps children born with a cleft – a split in the lip or roof of the mouth.

SMILE TRAIN HAS PAID FOR MORE THAN ONE MILLION OPERATIONS TO REPAIR CLEFTS.

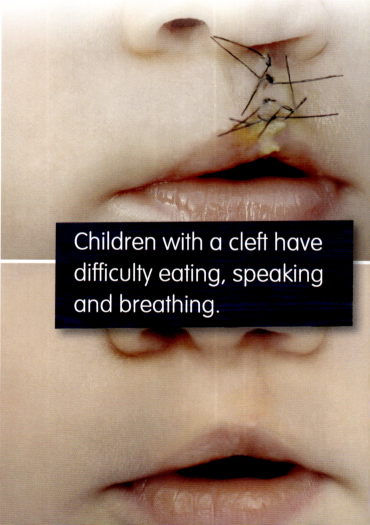

Children with a cleft have difficulty eating, speaking and breathing.

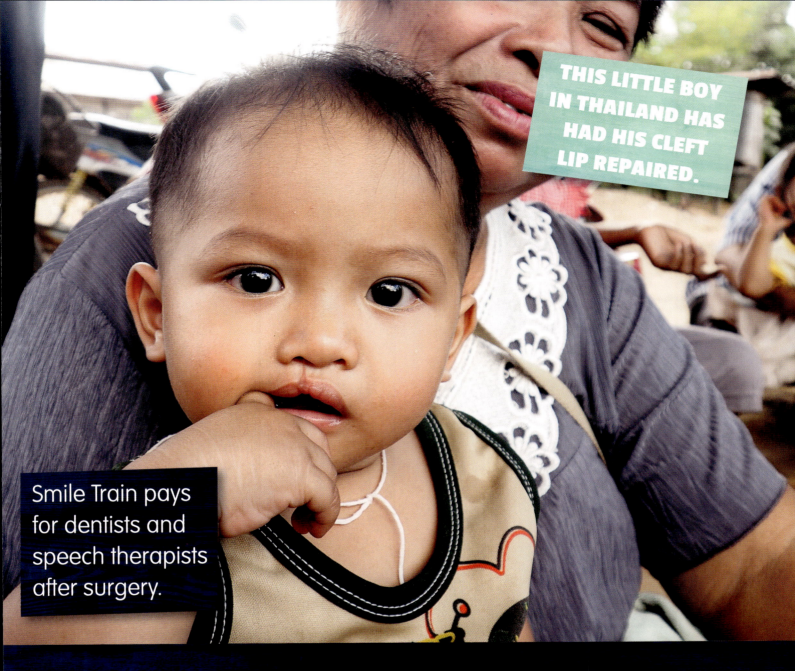

THIS LITTLE BOY IN THAILAND HAS HAD HIS CLEFT LIP REPAIRED.

Smile Train pays for dentists and speech therapists after surgery.

Smile Train supports research around the world into why clefts happen. It also educates people about some of the causes of the problem.

# HEART HEALTH

**EIGHT OUT OF TEN BABIES BORN WITH A HEART DEFECT NOW SURVIVE.**

Many babies are born with serious health problems. Heart problems are the most common. Research is helping doctors diagnose and treat these problems.

Many people with heart disease need a life-saving **heart transplant**. Medical research has made transplants possible. Globally, more than 5,000 are now carried out each year.

The first heart transplant was carried out in 1967.

British Heart Foundation

CHARITIES LIKE THE BRITISH HEART FOUNDATION SUPPORT RESEARCH INTO HEART DISEASE.

# HOW YOU CAN HELP

Ask an adult to help you find out about the work of a charity. Then ask family members if they could make a regular donation.

Ask your parents about sponsored family events in your area.

THIS ANNUAL SPONSORED RUN RAISES MONEY FOR A CANCER CHARITY.

**DONATED ITEMS CAN BE SOLD BY A CHARITY TO RAISE MONEY.**

You can also help charities by giving your time instead of money.

Are you are lucky enough to receive birthday and Christmas gifts? Some people ask for donations to a charity instead of presents for themselves.

# FUND RAISING

## BE A CHARITY SUPERHERO

You could raise money by selling drinks and snacks.

INVENT YOUR OWN SUPERHERO OR DRESS UP AS SPIDER-MAN OR BATGIRL.

Why not organise a charity superheroes disco at school?
Ask everyone, including teachers, to come dressed as
a superhero and donate the entry fee!

What jobs could you do at home? Ask your parents to pay you a small amount each time you help. Give the money to charity.

WASHING DISHES COULD HELP YOUR PARENTS AND A CHARITY TOO!

# GLOSSARY

| | |
|---|---|
| **cancer** | a serious disease that can affect different parts of the body |
| **causes** | issues that people are concerned about and want to support |
| **cystic fibrosis** | a disease that affects the lungs and digestive system (how the body deals with food) |
| **diagnose** | decide which disease someone has |
| **donations** | things that are given to a charity, especially money |
| **drug companies** | companies that discover, make and sell medicines |
| **heart transplant** | an operation in which doctors remove a person's sick heart and replace it with a healthy heart |
| **laboratories** | rooms with special equipment where scientists carry out experiments |
| **organisation** | a group of people, such as a club or charity, with a particular purpose |
| **profit** | money made by a business after all its costs have been paid |
| **research** | tests and experiments carried out by scientists to find out new information |
| **treatments** | medicine, or sometimes other methods, used to help cure a disease or heal an injury |

# INDEX